HANDBOOKS OF EUROPEAN NATIONAL DANCES

EDITED BY
VIOLET ALFORD

DANCES OF DENMARK

Plate 1
Himmerland

DANCES *of* DENMARK

POUL LORENZEN
and
JEPPE JEPPESEN

NOVERRE PRESS

ILLUSTRATED BY
ROWLAND A. BEARD
ASSISTANT EDITOR
YVONNE MOYSE

First published in 1950
This edition published in 2021 by
The Noverre Press
Southwold House
Isington Road
Binsted
Hampshire
GU34 4PH

ISBN 978-1-906830-98-4

Illustrations in Colour, pages 2, 12, 29, 39
Map of Denmark, page 6

INTRODUCTION

T̲H̲E̲ oldest and most widely-
spread European dance must certainly be the Chain dance.
We see it in ancient Greece circling the orchestra of the
early Greek theatre, and can follow it into modern Greece,
where—to name the best-known—as the Kalamatianos it
rings the village dancing-place to the present day.* As
the Carole it attained extraordinary popularity all through
the Middle Ages, and although England, France and Italy
contribute much to our knowledge of it, it is Denmark
which supplies the most detailed information of this ever-
living Chain. The riches of Danish balladry mention it
again and again as the Ring dance, which, opening, becomes the Chain. In this small northern country it seems
to have been the principal dance at court, castle and manor.
As to the peasant people, we suppose they too enjoyed it,
for the division between gentry and villagers becomes less
and less the farther one goes back in social life, before the
rise of the burgesses and rich middle class.

Danish ballads deal romantically with Kings and Prin-
cesses, with Knights and Squires—a Swain, a country
gentleman below a Knight in rank, is the most modest
person mentioned as a rule. They do not tell us what the
country folk were doing, nor the fisher-folk, nor the crafts-
men in the towns. A fresco on the wall of Orslev church,
on the island of Zealand, dating from about A.D. 1400,
shows a Chain dance by nine people, three of whom are
ladies, the leader and the last man carrying rosettes or

* See *Dances of Greece* in this series.

tight, round bouquets. This is as widely-spread a practice as the dance itself, and flowered sticks, ribboned wands, or bouquets are carried as insignia of office wherever the Chain winds its way.

In Denmark the leader also led the ballad to which they danced—ballads of interminable length, telling stories of Kings and Queens, tragic, romantic, quasi-historical. The King looked out of his window in his ' tower strong ' and heard the sound of dancing and singing. He asks:

> Who is yon Knight who leads the dance,
> And louder than all the song he chants?*

Another ballad tells of the King's daughter who led the Round in song. Knowledge of the dance and a good memory were equally necessary for a leader, for all depended on him or her for figures and words. As well as bouquets we are shown the leader bearing a silver cup as sign of office—perhaps snatched from the banqueting table.

> There dances Sir Stig, as light as a wand,
> With a silver cup in his white hand.†

Often the Knights danced with drawn swords in their hands—not a Hilt-and-Point Sword dance, but as a mark of their rank and to ' honour the maidens '.

> There danced the Knights of pride
> With swords drawn by their sides,‡

and as in other countries, the churchyard was often the chosen spot for the Chain dance.

> Gay went the dance in the kirkyard there,
> There danced Knights with sword-blades bare,
> There danced the maidens with hair unbound,
> It was the King's daughter sang the Round.§

Another ballad gives a picture of dancers bearing torches and garlands of red roses, akin, one supposes, to the old

---

* A. Olrik : *A Book of Danish Ballads,* 1939.
† Prof. J. Steenstrup : *The Medieval Popular Ballad* (trans. E. G. Cox). 1891.   ‡ Olrik, *op. cit.*   § Olrik, *op. cit.*

Norwegian Kyndledans, a wedding ceremony in which these objects were carried; but in Denmark it must have been a Chain dance, for a Knight led it and sang the song.

✤ THE BEGGAR DANCE ✤

Two other dances are named in ballads, the Lucky Dance and the Beggar Dance, both of which appear to have been Chain forms. The story of Proud Signelil and Queen Sophie tells us:

> When to the castle gate she chanced
> She saw them dancing the Beggar Dance.
> Twice they danced the dance around,
> The Queen stood gazing at her spellbound.*

The Beggar Dance was popular in Holstein also—the German province bordering the Danish frontier—and was still used there for weddings in 1886, with miming and Rounds, while the unedifying story of the Beggarman and the village wife was popular as a ballad all over the North from the sixteenth century at least. The Gaberlunzie Man of James V of Scotland, supposed to have been written, and indeed enacted many a time, by the King himself incognito, bears a strong resemblance to this Holstein Beggar. This was but one of the Beggar ballads of Scotland 'too licentious to be admitted' to the famous Percy collection.

✤ THE LUCKY DANCE ✤

The Lucky Dance proved anything but lucky to the maidens who trod it, and ended in tragedy when they stepped

> . . . so lightly o'er the lea
> When the King of the Wends with all his ships
> Came sailing in from sea,†

and carried away two of the maidens to his Wendish kingdom up the Baltic. Today on the Faroe Islands we

* Steenstrup, *op. cit.* † Olrik, *op. cit.*

can see the Chain dance still circling to its ballad sung by the dancers, and but yesterday in the Ringköbing district of West Jutland a Chain called Tospring (Two-spring) was done at peasant weddings.

☙ THE FAROE CHAIN DANCE ❧

The Faroe islanders link their chains especially on the National Festival, July 29th, on Midsummer Day and on long winter evenings when people go to each other's houses for company and cheer. One man will rise and begin the ballad, another joins him, two or three more, and the chain begins its clockwise circle. The house door is pushed open, people look in, then eagerly find a place in the chain which joins up into a ring. More and more come in, so that the leader breaks the ring and re-forms it as a double chain. When the floor is packed to its limits the ring has burst out into small bulges, looped so that part of the chain is dancing back to back. The step is very simple and there is no room to do more than sketch it, almost on the spot. It is a step, *ensemble*, twice to the left, once to the right, while the arms, with a good hand grip, move backwards and forwards with energetic jerks. Musical instruments are never used and apparently never have been; sung ballads are innumerable, the earliest dating from about 1300, although the first account of the Faroe chain dance is from the seventeenth century only.*

☙ THE PAIR DANCE ARRIVES ❧

But communications became easier, and fashions from other countries spread to the North. The Pair dance arrived, horrified the older generation but took a firm

* See *E.F.D.S. Journal*, 1928, No. 2: extract from *Folkesangen paa Færöerne* by H. Thuren, 1908. [*Note.*—The foregoing paragraphs of the Introduction have been contributed by the Editor.]

hold on social dancing, and the antique Chain dropped out except in out-of-the-way places. The Minuet arrived about 1700, was taught by fashionable dancing-masters throughout the eighteenth and early nineteenth centuries, went out of fashion, but the name was retained and is still carried on by the folk, although the dance itself has undergone a sea change, and is today a figure dance of the Country Dance type. The Viennese Waltz arrived about 1800. Polka and Mazurka came from Central Europe about 1845. These, in the usual shuttle movement, came from the folk of their various countries to flourish awhile in ball-rooms, vanished before the shuffling, slip-slip-slipping dances from America, to return to the folk —the Danish folk this time. Every northern country has thus welcomed them (with the exception of Great Britain, whose dances are certainly much less influenced since they have, as a rule, kept their Country dance forms though Polka steps crept in). Their very names show their origins. In Denmark, besides the three just mentioned, there are the Polonaise, Varsovienne, Anglaise, Française, the Hamburger, the Holstein Waltz and the Rhinelander. These, discarded as ball-room dances, are faithfully preserved by the peasant people, and some have been practised up to these days with gusto. They were and are danced all over the country in various forms, though sometimes under different names. The only purely local dance now known is the Sönderhoning, the dance from Sönderho, a Fanö town.

OPPOSITION TO DANCING

Even the old communal Chain, with men and women merely holding hands, had given great offence to the Reformed Church. A preacher proclaimed it 'a circle whose centre is the devil himself, and whose participants are dancing towards eternal death'. This was the attitude of mind that gave rise to the horrific tale of the dancers of

Plate 2
Randers, Jutland

Kolbigk who, on that eleventh-century Christmas morning, impatiently stamped in the churchyard while Mass was being celebrated. So impatient were they that they began to Carole before the Office was finished and were condemned to encircle the churchyard for a year as their punishment. Just such a fanatically prejudiced spirit was alive in England, when the writer of that strangely puritanical work two hundred years or so before the Puritans, which he called *Handling Sin*, declaimed about the self-same dance:—

> Daunces, Karole and Somour Games,
> Of many swych come many shames.

Yet the dance was performed by men and women guests in the monastery of Eskilsö at Yuletide, by invitation of the monks themselves. It is true it circled only round the refectory table, but the Bishop felt he must put a stop to such an unseemly performance.

When the Pair dances arrived one can imagine the scandal. One denouncement proclaimed: ' One would think these dancers had bitten the head off all shame, and that they had become completely insane.' How many voices have screamed out words of that sort all over Europe and about all sorts of dances, from the Rigaudon of Provence to the Waltz of Vienna?

Let us return to the Polka, that gay couple dance from Poland, or perhaps Czechoslovakia—for they claim it too —which burst into scandalised European ballrooms. A curious fact is that a dance named Polsk-dance reached Denmark at least 200 years before London artists were caricaturing Polka couples twirling between heavy Victorian tables and chairs, coat-tails flying, crinolines billowing, wearied pianists thumping on spindly upright pianos. As early as 1647 Bishop Hans Michelsen of Fyn (Funen)—a Bishop of different calibre from the one who ruled over the monks of Eskilsö—married his two sons at a double wedding in the Council House at Odense. Amongst the wedding dances the Polsk-dance already figured, and the Right Reverend Bishop saw no ill in himself dancing a turn with each of the brides. This Polsk, however, although a Pair dance, must not be wholly identified with the Polka, for it contained a march forward and a turning on the spot. It was probably the same dance which developed into the large and ornate Country-dance figures of the Swedish and Finnish Polskas for four or more couples.*

A comparatively modern dance, the Svejtritt, even had a new ballad made upon it—not to be danced to, but to teach a frightful lesson. At a ball at Horsens they danced the Svejtritt for the first time—

> They danced for three mortal hours,
> They danced and did not cease;
> Fainting they fell on the floor,
> Fell down and died, every one.
> Yes, they fell down and died
> And they never rose up again!

Would the dancers of Kolbigk have preferred that to their year's punishment followed by St. Vitus dance?

⚜ MEN'S DANCES ⚜

Denmark possesses a Stick dance for two men facing one another. They each hold a stout stick in either hand, and clash them together under each knee in turn and in every conceivable position. Besides this, which is a common European dance, we may mention Karlenes Fornöjelse, The Farm Lads' Pleasure, and Törvedansen, The Peat Dance. These are not in the category of men's ritual dances for they belong to no marked season or day, but there is one at least, which must once have had a ritual or magical intention. This is the Millwheel Dance,† Bette

* See *Dances of Sweden* and *Dances of Finland* in this series.
† See *Dances of Switzerland* in this series for another example.

Mand ud aa æ Horhied, from the district of Salling. One variant is done by four, or preferably six men. They hold each other by the hand, and using an ordinary running step, run round in a ring. Alternate men then allow themselves to slide towards the middle, heels together, toes pointed, until they are practically lying feet meeting in the middle. They are supported by the firm grip of the other three who continue to circle round, pulling the first three round as they lie. Then they change places, the lying men leaping up while the running men in their turn allow their feet to slide to the middle and are swirled round. The change-over must be exceedingly smart and precise, and is repeated every eight bars, until the men have had enough. Finally, on the last eighth bar they stop. Those lying down turn a back somersault, still supported by the tautly stretched arms of the standing three; these then take their turn at a back somersault. The dance is violent, and if a man bears another a grudge he can loose his hand-grip and drop his enemy most unpleasantly.

THE DANCE TODAY

As in all Scandinavian countries the Maypole is still raised, and dancing round it or the living Midsummer tree is still performed. But no special dances are prescribed. This ancient rite is now an amusement and a social meeting only. All the important occasions in the life of the people are marked by feasting and dancing. They dance or danced at christenings, at weddings, at the Church festivals, at the harvest feasts, even at funerals.

We must acknowledge that most of our dances today date only from the middle of the eighteenth century to about the middle of the nineteenth. The folk dance revival in Denmark is being carried on largely by Foreningen til Folkedansens Fremme, the Danish Association for the Promotion of Folk Dance. This was founded as early as 1901, so has half a century of work behind it, and has given birth to many other associations, large and small, all over the country. These have now combined to form the national organisation called simply Danske Folke-dansere, Danish Folk Dancers. The enormous number of 1,000 dances have been collected and recorded, and a history of Danish folk dance is now being compiled.

✤ MUSIC ✤

The dance tunes of Denmark are numberless. Up to 10,000 have been found in old music books belonging to village fiddlers, and they are as heterogeneous as the men who so painstakingly wrote them down. The old books themselves are of interest, from those in good leather bindings with gold lettering, down to those in covers of brown paper which had once contained a pound of finest Dutch canaster—a favourite tobacco. Some are beautifully preserved, some almost undecipherable; rings from beer mugs and coffee cups and punch have marked them. But when they are made to deliver up their contents, the pleasure enjoyed by our countryfolk for the hundred years between, say, 1750 and 1850 can be our pleasure today.

Village fiddlers are no professionals, so the notation is often difficult to read; but that was of small moment to the writers who had the tunes safe in their memories, and only needed a glance at the score. Like the influx of dances when the old Chain broke, most of the tunes are from abroad. But the conservation by a conservative peasantry has at length turned them into Danish traditional tunes. The more they are studied the more clearly does it appear that the great majority were used all over the country, and cannot be claimed as a local possession anywhere. There are, of course, a few exceptions to prove this rule.

' It is interesting ', says a Danish music expert, ' to

observe how extremely unpopular is this opinion. Many people feel quite aggrieved on learning that their own traditional dance is known elsewhere.' He adds: ' Danish traditional music, when compared with that of some neighbouring countries, is wonderfully unspoiled. Too much handling and adaptation evolves an artificial product, but to me our own folk music seems like a bunch of wild flowers with the dew still on them.'

COSTUME

There are still many regional costumes worn throughout Denmark on great occasions, and the revival which has been going on in traditional dance and music is helping towards recovery in the wearing of them. None can be claimed as national, for they vary from district to district, from island to island, even from village to village, especially as regards women's headgear.

Fanö Island, west of Jutland, and Læsö in the Kattegat, east of Jutland, still show their women's costumes. This last island possesses a large white folded scarf as headdress of medieval aspect, many silver chains and ornaments and—of old—solid silver belts of linked oblong pieces. Fishwomen from Skovshoved may be seen in Copenhagen in full costume.

The Fanö costumes are interesting, red frieze skirts for old women, myrtle-green for young ones: on the right side of the bodice from neck to waist and at the wrists black velvet bands woven with flowers; large aprons almost like a second skirt, and shoulder kerchiefs, with the point in front instead of at the back, are crossed at the neck and the ends fastened on either shoulder with pins. Kerchiefs are red check on navy for joy, blue or green check on navy for mourning. Buttons are of amber or silver, on the left of the skirt and on the right side of the bodice.

The head-dress is multiple: a white cotton square folded diagonally and fastened at the nape of the neck, no hair showing. Above this a cap of white gathered into the nape by a tape, and stuffed with horsehair into a crown on the top of the head. Even this is not enough, for an outer kerchief, matching the shawl, covers all; folded diagonally, the point is placed on the top of the head over the stuffed-out crown, and fastened at the nape. The rest of the kerchief is pulled over the forehead, the ends passed round the head, right-hand end on top, forward to front and tied once so that the left-hand end stands up vertically above the other.

And even this is not sufficient protection against the sand-drift from the west. When this blows up the *strud* goes on, a mask of black cloth lined with cotton stuff and bound with patterned cotton. It is made in two parts which join across the nose and at the temples.

The 'tucking-band' also belongs to Fanö, a red and blue woollen band with big tassels. It goes round the figure below the hips, and the voluminous skirts can be hoisted up by it out of the wet.

The men nearly all went to sea and learned to dress like townspeople when ashore. A yellow silk waistcoat, however, indicated that the wearer had crossed the Equator.

Himmerland, Jutland. The type of costume illustrated dates from about 1840. The woman's very full red frieze skirt is bound with red braid and has two bands of pale-blue taffeta ribbon at prescribed intervals from the hem. The bodice, red also, is of linsey-woolsey with narrow vertical stripes of black wool or unbleached thread. Its basque is bound with pale-blue ribbon. The front of the bodice is stiffened with whalebone and laced up tightly, while the sleeves are not of the linsey-woolsey but knitted in red wool and sewn in. The apron is woollen also, striped on a black ground and gathered into a hand-woven multi-coloured waistband tied in front. Married women wear black bonnets, girls one of white taffeta, the back piece heavily embroidered with flowers, while a brown silk folded square goes round the edge of the bonnet to be fastened with pins on the top of the head and behind the ears. A bow of brocaded ribbon covers the tape which goes under the chin, and an amusing detail is the three glass beads which conceal the tape.

The man wears tight white breeches with silver buckles at the knee, a woollen waistcoat with stripes and an old-fashioned upstanding collar. Under the collar, a brown square, like that round the woman's bonnet, is used in place of a tie, knotted in front so that the ends stand well out. A short jacket of navy-blue frieze reaches a little below the waist, with silver buttons, as has the waistcoat. Multi-coloured garters are tied below the knee on the outside of the leg, and the shoes have handsome silver buckles. The red stocking-cap boasts a tassel and a brushed-up fluffy border.

❦ *NOTE* ❧

The costumes of Denmark are greatly prized by their owners. Dancers wear their own local costumes, so in modern dance gatherings all sorts of costumes may be seen in the same dance. If you attempt to copy the costumes illustrated here, do so seriously, without introducing your own fancies.

The Editor

SOME OCCASIONS WHEN DANCING MAY BE SEEN

Midsummer Day, June 24th	Chain dances, Faroe Islands.
The National Festival, July 29th	Thorshavn, Faroes, for three days.
Every two weeks during summer	Frilands Museum, Lyngby near Copenhagen. Costume displays.

FOLK DANCE GROUPS

Danske Folkedansere (Danish Folk Dancers). Address: Hr. Forstander Thyregaard, Sallings Ungdomsskolebjerg. The national organisation combining nearly all groups.

Foreningen til Folkedansens Fremme (The Danish Folk Dance Association). Address: Frk. Aase Meier, Birkholmsvej 7, Holte, Copenhagen.

Aalborgegnens Folkedansere, Aalborg.

Odense Folkedansere, Odense.

Aarhus og Omegns Folkedansere, Aarhus.

Horsens Folkedanseforening, Horsens.

Holstebro Folkedanseforening, Holstebro.

Sönderborg Amts Folkedansere, Sönderborg.

Randers Amts Folkedansere, Randers.

Randers Bys Folkedansere, Randers.

THE DANCES

TECHNICAL EDITORS
MURIEL WEBSTER AND KATHLEEN P. TUCK

ᴴᴴᴴᴴᴴᴴᴴ

ABBREVIATIONS
USED IN DESCRIPTION OF STEPS AND DANCES

r—right ⎤ referring to
l—left ⎦ hand, foot, etc.

C—clockwise

R—right ⎤ describing turns or
L—left ⎦ ground pattern

C-C—counter-clockwise

For descriptions of foot positions and explanations of any ballet terms the following books are suggested for reference:

A Primer of Classical Ballet (Cecchetti method). Cyril Beaumont.

First Steps (R.A.D.). Ruth French and Felix Demery.

The Ballet Lover's Pocket Book. Kay Ambrose.

Reference books for description of figures:

The Scottish Country Dance Society's Publications. Many volumes, from Thornhill, Cairnmuir Road, Edinburgh 12.

The English Folk Dance and Song Society's Publications. Cecil Sharp House, 2 Regent's Park Road, London, N.W.1.

The Country Dance Book I–VI. Cecil J. Sharp. Novello & Co., London.

The poise of body is very upright, and in the turns the dancers lean back from one another.

In line formation both hands are free and hang loosely to the sides. In couple dancing, inside hands are joined, outside hands free.

Waltz Grasp. The man puts his r arm round the woman's waist and grasps her r hand with his l, keeping it at shoulder height. The woman places her l hand on the man's r shoulder from behind.

Arming is done with either r or l arm; the joined arms are strongly bent, the other arm is free.

Cross Grasp. Partners cross hands in front, taking r hand in r, and l hand in l; partners either facing each other or side by side.

Waist Grasp. In couples or in a circle. The men grasp the women's waists and the women put their hands on the men's shoulders.

Shoulder Grasp. The dancers place their hands on each other's shoulders.

Swing. Dancing round in circles, mills, or with own partner on spot, when the first part of the music is used. Dancing round in couples can be done either on the spot (C or C-C), round the room, or round the set. If nothing else is stated, the couples move round the room in the usual direction (C-C) and turn round C. Turning round C-C is called the reverse turn.

Circle. This is formed by a number of dancers, joining hands if not otherwise stated.

Big Circle. A circle in which all the dancers join.

One-handed Mill is formed by four or more dancers grasping each other's r hands (straight arm) or the wrist of the one in front, thumbs pointing upwards, dancing round C; or grasping each other's l hands when dancing round C-C.

Two-handed Mill is formed by four dancers. Two of the dancers, who stand opposite each other, grasp each other's hands (r with l, l with r). The two others, who also stand opposite each other, take the same grasp but put their r arm from above through the ring formed by the first two dancers and the l arm from below. The arms are kept straight. In mills, circles and other figures, where one first dances C and then C-C, the turn is often marked with an ' appel ' (stamp).

Gate. Two dancers raise their inside hands which are joined, thus forming an arch under which the dancers may pass.

Chain. This is done in a circle formed by couples. If nothing else is stated, the man takes his partner's r hand in his own r, then the next woman's l hand in his l. The men pass round C, the women C-C. Other kinds of chains are described in the various dances.

Turns are made towards the centre, when dancing in a circle or quadrille.

N.B.—In ' tur ' dances (figure dances) the dancers themselves decide how many of the figures they wish to dance.

BASIC STEPS

Walking, running, polka, waltz, gallop and skipping steps are commonly used and need no description.

Appel
   A stamp on one foot, often used at the beginning of a series of walking or skipping steps.

Hopsa   Beats
   A turning step, usually done with a partner and sometimes described as ' Spring Waltz ' or turning Pas de Basque.

23

Spring on l foot, turning to R.   I
Step on r foot.   and
Close l foot beside r (half-turn has now been   2
completed.)
Spring on r foot, turning to R.   I
Step on l foot   and
Close r foot beside l. (A whole turn has   2
now been completed.)

WOMAN'S STEP
The same beginning with r foot.

Tyroler Hopsa

Pas de Basque rhythm (modified Pas de
Basque sauté).
Partners join inside hands and dance 4 Pas de   8 bars
Basque moving away, towards, away and   of 2/4
towards partner.
Partners then join with Waltz grasp and
dance 4 Hopsa steps, turning to the R.
Man starts with l, woman with r foot.

Tyroler Waltz (modified Pas de Basque glissé).
As Tyroler Hopsa, but with a step instead   8 bars
of a spring on the first beat, making the   of 3/4
whole movement smoother: i.e. 4 Balancé
steps followed by 4 Waltz steps turning.

Hurré or Gammelmands (Old Man's Step).
This is the name given to the Hurré step in the Himmerland. The actual step is a pivot step and may be danced
with a partner holding Waltz grasp. When turning C,
the weight is on the r foot on every beat and the l foot
is used on the 'and' beat to push off. The counting
would be '*right* and *right* and *right*', etc. The r foot
hardly moves from the original position, as the movement is a turning one, not a travelling one. When

24

danced in a circle travelling C, the r foot is placed in the centre and the l foot kept behind the r, the dancers leaning back and allowing the r foot to travel to L as little as possible. When danced C-C the weight is on the l foot.

	Beats
Chassé. A Polka step without a hop.	
Step forward l.	1
Close r behind l foot.	and
Step forward l foot.	2
Repeat, beginning with the r foot.	1 and 2

French Reel Step	
Step and hop on l foot, circling the r leg (forwards sideways backwards).	1 and
Step on r foot immediately behind the l foot;	2
hop on r foot, circling l leg.	and
The step is done on the spot, the circling foot taking the place of the hopping foot.	

Two-Step.   A quick turn on alternate feet.
Partners hold with ordinary Waltz grasp and, leaning away from one another, travel C-C round the room or set, but revolving C as in the ordinary Waltz.   The feet are slightly apart, first the woman stepping between the man's feet with her r foot, while the man steps round on his l foot.   Then the man steps between her feet with his r foot, while she steps round him with l foot.   The rhythm is steady—1 2, 1 2.

	Beats
Mazurka Step (Danish Mazurka step, not to be confused with the Polish step of the same name).	
Step forward on r foot.	1
Close l foot up behind r foot in 3rd position.	2
Hop on l foot, swinging r leg forward and	and
then bending the lower leg slightly towards the l knee.	3

25

TO TING (*Two Things*)

⚜

Region	Himmerland. Plate 1.	

Character   Variation of 2/4 and 3/4 tempo gives contrasting smooth and springy movements.

Formation   Couple dance.   Travel C-C.

Dance	MUSIC *Bars*
FIGURE I	**A**
a Partners hold inside hands, other hands free; start with outside feet.	1–4
4 Tyroler Waltz steps dancing away, towards, away and towards partner.	
b 4 Tyroler Waltz steps turning with usual Waltz grasp.	5–8
Repeat I*a* and I*b*.	1–8
FIGURE II	**B**
a 4 Tyroler Hopsa steps, grasp as in I*a*.	9–12
b 'Two-step', turning partner with Waltz grasp.	13–16
Repeat II*a* and II*b*.	9–16

TO TING

From Himmerland
Arranged by Arnold Foster

OTTE MANDS DANS (*Eight Men's Dance*)

Region   Himmerland. Plate 1.

Character   Lively.

Formation   Four couples in square formation (○=woman, □=man):

Dance	MUSIC *Bars*
FIGURE I	
a Circle	A
Hands joined in circle; 8 walking steps C-C, with Appel (stamp) on the first.	1–4
8 walking steps C with Appel (stamp) on the first.	1–4
b Cross-over (chorus figure which is repeated after each step).	B
1st couple crosses through 4th couple while 2nd couple crosses through 3rd, i.e. couple on the L. The woman crosses between the man and woman while her partner moves behind the woman on his left and then through the middle, so that the woman crosses first; the step used for	5–12

Plate 3
Hedebo, Zealand

cross-over is 3 chassés (beginning on l foot) and 2 walking steps; partners meet in opposite place and with ordinary Waltz grasp turn with Gammelmands step, the man finishing with 3 stamps.

At the same time, 3rd and 4th couples open for cross-over, with one chassé forward and 2 walking steps, the woman moving obliquely forward to her R, the man to his L.

3rd and 4th couples close with the same step, moving backward; they stand still during the Gammelmands step.

1st and 2nd couples repeat the cross-over through the couple now on their L and turn in original places.

3rd and 4th couples now dance the cross-over and turn in opposite places.

3rd and 4th couples now dance the cross-over and turn in own places.

1st and 2nd couples repeat the cross-over through the couple now on their L and turn in original places.	5–12
3rd and 4th couples now dance the cross-over and turn in opposite places.	5–12
3rd and 4th couples now dance the cross-over and turn in own places.	5–12

FIGURE II

a All four couples dance Gammelmands step, turning partners on the spot.

b Chorus (cross-over figure) as before.

	A
	1–4 (twice)
	B
	5–12 (4 times)

FIGURE III

a *Women's One-Hand Mill*
Women join r hands, 8 skips C.
Women join l hands, 8 skips C-C.
The hands are held high.

b Chorus.

	A
	1–4
	1–4
	B
	5–12 (4 times)

From Himmerland
Arranged by Arnold Foster

Play A *music twice,* B *music four times, for each figure.*
Add another A *music twice to end the dance.*

FIGURE IV

a *Men's Two-Hand Mill* (see Hand Grasps).
8 skips C.
8 skips C-C.

b Chorus.

A
1–4
(twice)

B
5–12
(4 times)

	A
FIGURE V	
a *Women's Two-Hand Mill*	1–4
8 skips C.	(twice)
8 skips C-C.	**B**
b Chorus.	5–12
	(4 times)
FIGURE VI	
a *Women's Wheel* (women's circle with shoulder grasp).	**A**
	1–4
8 skips C.	(twice)
8 skips C-C.	**B**
b Chorus.	5–12
	(4 times)
FIGURE VII	
a *Men's Wheel* (men's circle with shoulder grasp).	**A**
	1–4
8 skips C.	(twice)
8 skips C-C.	**B** ·
b Chorus.	5–12
	(4 times)
FIGURE VIII	**A**
a *Big Circle* (all hands joined in circle).	1–4
8 skips C.	(twice)
8 skips C-C.	**B**
b Chorus.	5–12
	(4 times)
FIGURE IX	**A**
a Partners turn each other with Gammelmands step.	1–4
	(twice)
(*b* is not danced after this figure, the dance always finishing with Gammelmands step.)	

FIRETUR (*Four Dance*)

᚛᚜᚛᚜

Region	From Jutland. Plates 2 and 3.
Character	Spirited.
Formation	Set of two couples facing one another, men on L of women.

Dance	MUSIC *Bars*
FIGURE 1	
a Circle	A
Hands joined in circle. 8 skips C, 8 skips C-C.	1–8
b Chassé	B
Partners face each other and change places with their side partner, women going in front of men, with 2 chassé steps sideways ; all dance 6 snatch or retiré steps on spot, facing own partner.	9–12
Repeat the chassé steps back to place, women still passing in front of men ; 6 retiré steps on the spot.	13–16
c Arm Hook Chain	A
All link r arm with opposite partner and turn for 4 walking steps.	1–8
Repeat with own partner for 8 walking steps.	
Repeat with opposite partner for 4 walking steps.	
d Two-Step	B
Couples hold each other by waist and travel C-C round set, turning partner with Two-step.	9–16

FIGURE II

a   One-Hand Mill
  With r hands joined in wheel, 8 skips C.
  With l hands joined in wheel, 8 skips C-C.

A
1–8

b, c, d Chorus, as in Figure I.

B A B

FIGURE III

a   Two-Hand Mill
  One couple joins both hands, the other couple joining hands with the r hand above, and the l hand below, the joined hands.
  8 skips C.   8 skips C-C.

A
1–8

b, c, d Chorus.

B A B

FIGURE IV

a   Goose-Walk
  Dancers move C-C in single file for 8 walking steps.   Repeat, moving C.

A
1–8

b, c, d Chorus.

B A B

FIGURE V

a   Yoke (Basket as in American Square Dancing).
  The two men join hands and raise them over the heads of the women, who pass under, join hands with one another, and raise their arms over the men's heads and retain their grasped hands behind the men's shoulders. The men's hands are grasped behind the women's backs.
  8 skips C-C.   8 skips C.
  Note.—Hurré or Gammelmands step is sometimes used instead of skipping step.

A
1–8

b, c, d Chorus.

B A B

FIGURE VI

  Circle (as in Figure I*a*).
  N.B.—No Chorus after this Figure.

A
1–8

34

FIRETUR

From Jutland
Arranged by Arnold Foster

*The whole tune is played twice through for each figure
except the last, when A only is played*

SÖNDERHONING (*The Sönderho Dance*)

Region   Island of Fanö.   Plate 4.

Character   The movement is undulating and supposed to resemble the waves of the sea. The rhythm is unusual, a three-step rhythm being danced to duple time.

Formation   Couple dance.

Dance	MUSIC
	Bars
FIGURE I	A
Couples, standing side by side, may link arms or join inside hands, but the original or old-time grasp is described:—	1–8
Woman's l arm is held horizontal, her fist closed, the man's r arm rests on the woman's lower arm.	
Couples promenade C-C with walking steps, either 16 or 32, depending on whether the A music is repeated or not. The step is rather slow.	
FIGURE II	B
Sönderho step. Woman's r hand is held in the man's l and placed on his l hip; his r hand is held high on the woman's back while her l hand is placed on his r shoulder-blade. The couples revolve C-C round the room with the following step. (Couples start sideways to line of dance.)	9–16

36

SÖNDERHONING

From Fanö
Arranged by Arnold Foster

Man's step

1 Step forward on l foot turning to R (to back to line of dance).	Beat 1
2 Swing r foot round and place it behind l, still turning to R on balls of both feet and lowering the heels on the end of the turn (to face line of dance).	2 and
3 Step forward on r foot, still turning to R, until a full turn is completed.	1

Woman's step

1 Step forward on r foot, between partner's feet, turning to R.	1
2 Close l foot up to r foot, step forward on r, still turning.	2 and
3 Step or spring sideways on l foot, turning to R, so that a whole turn is now completed. After the step or jump on l the r foot may close up to the l, but there is no transference of weight.	1

The Sönderho step is danced five times, i.e. five completed turns, and takes 8 bars of music. Thus every second step begins on the last beat of a musical bar while every first, or odd, step begins on the first beat of a bar. The musical movement during this step should be continuous and smooth without any sudden change of speed, the man helping the woman round and lifting her if a jump is made. The jump varies according to how the music is played, but in every case the movement should have an undulating quality.

Repeat the whole dance.

N.B.—The man's step is similar to the step of the Swedish Hambo, and the woman's to that of the Polonaise Jysk paa Næsen (Danish), although the rhythm is different. The Sönderho step is not described in characteristic steps as the timing is peculiar to this dance.

Plate 4
Fanö Island

BIBLIOGRAPHY

BURCHENAL, ELIZABETH.—*Folk Dances of Denmark*. Schirmer, New York, 1915.

JÖRGENSEN, SVEND.—*Den Gamle Spillemand*. (The Old Fiddler.) In *Folkedansen i Danmark* (The Folk Dance in Denmark), vol. 4, 1946.

KRAMP, L.—*Lidt om danske Folkedragter*. (Something about Danish peasant costume.) In *Folkedansen i Danmark*.

NIELSEN, H. GRÜNER.—*Vore ældste Folkedanse: Langdans og Polskdans* (Our oldest dances: the Long Dance and the Polish Dance.) 1917.

NIELSEN, H. GRÜNER.—*Folkelig Vals.* (The Folk Waltz.) 1920.

NORDQVIST, ELSA.—*Danish Folk Dances : Old Himmerland Dances*. Published by English-Scandinavian Summer School. Hutchinson, Chatham, 1932.

OLRIK, AXEL.—*A Book of Danish Ballads*. (Extracted from vols. 1–11 of Svend Grundtvig's *Danmarks Gamle Folkeviser*.) New York, 1939.

STEENSTRUP, JOHANNES C.—*Vore Folkeviser fra Middelalderen*. 1891. (Translated by E. G. Cox as *The Medieval Popular Ballad*, Boston, 1914.)

VEDEL, KLAVS.—*Folkedansens Historie*. In *Folkedansen i Danmark*.

The following may all be obtained from Foreningen til Folkedansens Fremme, Birkholmsvej 7, Holte, Copenhagen:

Musik til danske Folkedanse, 3 vols. *Beskrivelser af danske Folkedanse*, 3 vols. (Music and descriptions of Danish folk dances.)

12 Danish Folk Dances. (Violin score.)

Gamle Danse fra Fyn og Öerne. (Old dances from Funen and the Islands; 1 march. Violin score.)

Gamle Danse fra Randersegnen. (27 old dances from Randers and the vicinity; violin score.)

Legestuen. (The Nursery. 41 easy dances and 1 march, suitable for children.)